This book is a

From

_____

To

_____

Date

_____

THE POWER OF NETWORKING WITH PEOPLE

Lucky Okome

authorHOUSE®

AuthorHouse™ UK Ltd.
500 Avebury Boulevard
Central Milton Keynes, MK9 2BE
www.authorhouse.co.uk
Phone: 08001974150

Though this publication contains accurate information, it is sold with the understanding that the publisher is not engaged in rendering professional services. If professional advice or assistance is required, the service of a competent professional should be sought.

First published by AuthorHouse   03/26/2011

ISBN: 978-1-4567-7367-0

Any people depicted in stock imagery provided by Thinkstock are models, and such images are being used for illustrative purposes only.

Certain stock imagery © Thinkstock.

This book is printed on acid-free paper.
Because of the dynamic nature of the Internet, any Web addresses or links contained in this book may have changed since publication and may no longer be valid. The views expressed in this work are solely those of the author and do not necessarily reflect the views of the publisher, and the publisher hereby disclaims any responsibility for them.

QUOTE

"THE ONLY TRUE WISDOM IS IN
KNOWING YOU KNOW NOTHING"
Socrates

FOR FUNMI

YOU CONTINUE TO AMAZE AND INSPIRE
ME. THANK YOU FOR YOUR SACRIFICIAL
EXAMPLE OF MAKING OUR FAMILY YOUR
PRIORITY.

ACKNWOLEDGEMENTS

Special thanks to

The Chartered Institute of Marketing where I was taught how to network with people.

Members of the central working committee Manchester African Business Forum Limited for giving me the opportunity to develop and deliver a business talk on the power of networking - this was the inspiration to the birth of this book.

Pastor Ayoade Nath Ogundipe - You have constantly prayed for me and my family thereby making a positive impact in the life of my family.

The Sanusis, Jinadus, Akandes, Olawuyis, and the Odejimis - You believe in this message and in the messenger. I am grateful.

Professor John Obafunwa - Thank you for all the support and life line you have been giving me and my family. I will never forget.......

Oluwaseun Tobore and Oluwafemi Oghenekevwe - You bring me the greatest joy of my life. What a delight and privilege to be your dad.

Tajudeen Jinadu - Many thanks for being the gateway for my coming to the United Kingdom.

Oyetunji Oyenekan - You are an inspirational friend and hero, thanks

CONTENTS

FOREWORD

Interacting with people and building relationship can seem be doggy and probably difficult to acomplish.

Walking up to somebody you have not met before and starting a discussion that can lead to a relationship can be massively rewarding and enjoyable, but you can't relate to people successfully without taking some risks. The posibility of being turned down is enough to put you off, but every set back should be an opportunity to get back, learn from the experience and have another go.

I have never let any disappointment bring me down but rather see it as a blessing. I just put my energy and aspiration into moving on, believing that if one person turns me down another might accept me and be happy to talk to me.

Taking a risk is an inherent part of every endeavour especially in building a business and life relationship. Building relationship is a unique way of creating a fantastic atmosphere for yourself, your family, your business, your community and a nation as a whole. I have experienced the advantages of networking with people.

The power of networking with people will remind you of everything you need to consider – from the first charpter "getting ready" to the last will put you on the right track towards building a successful relationship in business and life. This book helps to illustrate step by step how to start and maintain a relationship for success in life.

It is a manual for those who cherish good relationship in Business, Management, Marketing, Banking and other sectors. To be truly successful in all aspects of life, you need to build relationship which can be possible through networking with people'.

I congratulate Lucky Okome for providing us with an easy to digest direction manual that shows us how to start, retain and maintain relationship in business and in life. For all those who need an exciting break through in business, using the power of networking, I recommend this book to you.

God bless you.
HRM Oba Joseph Adebayo Adewale JP OFR
The Owa Ajero of Ijero Kingdom

PREFACE

The power of networking is based on my experience at attending events organized by the Chartered Institute of Marketing here in the United Kingdom.

For many people, getting connected or close to people can seem pretty scary because they don't know what the consequences might be or probably because of fear. But from my experience, getting to know people can be massively rewarding and enjoyable.

As a new immigrant in the country, these events were eye openers and they gave me the opportunity of getting connected with my professional colleagues, students, and especially people that I might not be interested in getting close to.

I remember vividly that it was through these events that I got to know how to start my own business and know places in the United Kingdom.

THE BOOK

The power of networking will remind and show you everything you need to consider when networking with people from the first chapter, Getting prepared to Becoming a passionate net worker. This book is designed to do the following.

- To take you step by step through the stages of getting to know people.

- To help you identify the advantages of becoming a passionate net- worker.

- To create more business opportunity.

- To take your business to a greater height.

The chapters are arranged to take you through the various stages of achieving your aim of taking your business to the next level.

I have enjoyed writing this book and hope it is of help to you, the reader. Please act on the contents. It is not what you know that counts, but what you do with what you know.

Lucky Okome
August 2010

INTRODUCTION

Why this book? Why do we network? Million of books will be published this year, Why one more?

Permit me to give you just a little background on this noble topic.

Studies have shown that 80% of new businesses come from networking and meeting with people even for the first time, not to mention career opportunity.

WHY THIS BOOK?

I decided to write this book because many businesses have failed due to their inability or refusal to use the right management tool or professionals to aid and support the growth of their businesses. The biggest marketing and sales mistakes companies make is not to fully understand their market place i.e. applying marketing principles. People buy from or patronize a company to fulfill a need or desire and your market are closely linked to their fulfillment, sadly history is full of failed businesses because they do not understand their market place. In the ancient days, many carriage manufacturers went out of business because they failed to change by applying the principles of marketing. The first question a potential entrepreneur must answer is, "How do I get connected to customers for the sales of my product or services." The answer to this question is not far fetched as it is linked to networking and usually the foundation is through a marketing strategy.

In over a decade of my experience in coaching, mentoring, advising and helping new business entrepreneurs start and grow their businesses, I have found this to be the most important factor that determines the success or otherwise of a new business. Therefore, where do sales come from? The answer is, sales come from customers, customers from marketing, marketing comes from a strategy and a good strategy is networking with people.

A very good way of understanding strategic plans of networking is thus

Take a close look at a stair case that take you from one floor to the other in a building, usually it starts from the ground floor (zero level) and it takes you to the top floor, so it is with a good strategy as illustrated above.

Most people do not have the time for strategic plans when thinking of a new business. Their thinking is that, they don't need any strategy, because their business is too small or probably is too complicated for their type of business. This is a misconception of fact and a wrong way of doing business. A good networking is a fantastic strategy.

Almost everything that happens in a business transaction either comes from and or impacts on its strategy. For example, how information about the business will get to the public without extra cost, the contact person and probably a one to one introduction of the business profile can be done through networking with people.

WHY DO WE NETWORK?

There are different types of networking e.g. Computer networking, Social networking and Business networking, but the main issue in networking is increase in number through links. Networking in the field of computing is the practice of linking computer devices together to support digital communications among them. Social networking is a social structure made of individuals or organization called nodes which are tied (connected) by one or more specific type of interdependency such as friendship, kinship, common interest, financial exchange and dislike, relationship or beliefs, knowledge or prestige. Business networking is a powerful means of linking a business with other businesses thereby achieving a zero budget marketing plan. The emphasis here is on face to face communication and what actually happens during and after the meetings.

Well folks, everybody has the potential of becoming successful in business but this book could be an excellent tool to help you accelerate the process of achieving a 0% budget of marketing your product and services. The methods in this book have been tested and with my experience as a passionate net worker, I have journeyed towards an ever greater level of success, happiness, and fulfillments. I can honestly say that the power of networking will make your business grow and reach a new level of marketing your products and services.

This book can help you jumpstart your business, no matter the level your business is now, it will give your business cheap adverts, good public relations and awareness, face to face and one on one self exposure.

In a nut shell, this book gives you an innovative approach to a positive marketing strategy that will help make changes in your business. Add intention, expectation, determination, and persistence and you too can move your business forward by using the power of networking.

Lucky Okome

"A tree can not make a forest, get connected through networking with people and grow into forest"

CHAPTER ONE

GET READY AND BE PREPARED

I remember sometime ago that the word 'be prepared'is the motor that propelled the boys scout to readiness for action. Getting ready is an action for success and progress in life.

Getting prepared sometimes create a fearful situation which can be controlled by mere statements like "it is only your imagination don't worry, there is nothing to be afraid of" But you and I know this kind of fear medicine never really work, such soothing remark may give us fear relief for few minutes or may be a few hours, but the 'it is only in your imagination'treatment doesn't really build confidence and cure fear. However, fear is real and we must recognize the fact that it exists before we can conquer it.

Most fear today is psychological, worry, tension, embarrassment, panic,etc all stem from mismanaged, negative imaginations. But simply knowing the breeding ground of fear doesn't cure fear. If a physician discovers you have an infection in some part of your body, he proceeds with treatment to cure the infection. However 'it is only in your mind'treatment only shows that fear doesn't really exist, but it does. Fear is real, fear is success number one enemy, fear wears down physical vitality, fear actually makes people sick, shorten life and it closes your mouth when you want to speak and therefore makes it difficult for you to network.

Fear creates lack of confidence and that is why millions of people accomplish little and enjoy little because they couldn't network and move forward in their various businesses. Truly fear is a powerful force that must be tamed. Fears of all kinds and sizes are forms of psychological infections. If we cure a mental infection the same way we cure a body infection using specific and proven treatment, then fear can be cured.

To do this, first and foremost, though as part of your pre-treatment preparation, condition yourself with this fact 'that all confidence is acquired and developed. No one is born with confidence. Those people you know who radiate confidence, who have conquered worry, who are at ease every where and all the time acquired their confidence every bit of it. You too can, yes we can acquire confidence.

In other to conquer fear and worries, I have identified the following types of fear / worries and suggested actions to be taken to permanently put it into control.

1. FEAR OF PEOPLE: Put them in proper perspective. Remember, the other person is just another human being pretty much like you.

2. FEAR OF WHAT PEOPLE MAY THINK: Make sure that what you plan to do or say is right. Then do it and say it. No one ever does anything worthwhile for which he or she is not criticized.

3. FEAR OF LOSING AN IMPORTANT CUSTOMER: Make sure you are honest in your presentation of your business and work hard to give better products or services. Correct anything that may have caused customers to lose confidence in you.

4. EMBARRASMENT BECAUSE OF PERSONAL APPEARRANCE: Improve it, go to the saloon, buy nice but not expensive clothes and in general practice better grooming. It doesn't always take new clothes.

5. FEAR OF THINGS GOING BEYOND YOUR CONTROL: Usually, the thinking of people is that things could go the other way, but you can conquer this by switching your attention to something generally different from the main issue.

In conclusion make sure you arrive at every event, meeting, or business commitment feeling calm, friendly and full of confidence, know where you are going, for what time, with plenty of business card and complimentary flyers of your business.

"Opportunity eludes so many people because they look too far for it, get connected by networking with people and seize the opportunity."

CHAPTER TWO

Make the first move

If you don't make the move and show that you are interested in what you see in the environment you find yourself at a particular time, you may come away from an event or conference feeling that you have missed an opportunity because no one talks to you. It is your responsibility to make the first move in other to achieve the benefit of a good networking with people for your business.

The reality is that, you must provide the stability that you want in your business. The good news is that the more people know you and your product/service the more you will attract the clients, projects, resources, people, ideas, money, and opportunities that you want. The following suggestions will help you make the first move.

Firstly, when in a formal networking environment, make the first move in a friendly and helpful way. Be a welcoming stranger, adopt an attitude of enjoyment and help others feel at ease. Take the pressure off yourself to "sell", this will definitely not happen on a first encounter. The objective is to meet people for the joy of meeting people.

Secondly, always give people something that they can remember you by. It might seem easier to give them something tangible such as a business card. People will remember you on how you make them feel. As you meet people and engage with them, always leave them feel better about themselves by sharing a bit of good humor or by noticing something positive about them e.g. 'I love the color of your tie. Add value by demonstrating your knowledge and experience. A gadget will be quickly forgotten, but a positive experience stays in the memory for a long time.

Thirdly, ask questions to find out more about the other person. Remember you may need up to six encounters with someone before they truly understand you and build a level of trust. Propose various ways to stay committed over time so you can build a relationship with the person. Phone calls, e-mail, and probably coffee date are some of the medium you can use to build this relationship, ask for permission to follow up in a tangible way. For example '

can I give you a call on Thursday at 12.00noon lunch time to continue our conversation?'Obviously the answer will be yes or another appropriate time agreed.

Lastly, be a commenter by finding out what the other person value or needs most. The initial value you bring to a new person while networking, use it to help the person satisfy a priority need, especially one not directly related to what you offer. This will create a much stronger positive impression than trying to 'sell'yourself. It will also encourage a dynamic of generosity and openness.

"Do not sing, standing on the Promises, when all you are doing is sitting on the premises, go networking with people and get connected."

CHAPTER THREE

START WITH SMALL CONVERSATION

Starting a conversation can be one of the most stressful things in life but also one of the most rewarding. Some people make it seem effortless, they glide across a room and after just a few words, and they have kindled a warm conversation. Although one of the scariest part of meeting new people is trying to start a conversation but I feel it doesn't need to be so.

Starting a conversation is as easy as eating and breathing provided that you are not suffering from social anxiety disorder (SAD) which is known as having an irrational fear of being watched, judged, evaluate, embarrassed or humiliated. This anxiety and discomfort becomes so extreme that it interferes with your functioning- this can be managed.

Normally the person you are trying to start a conversation with, will have some jewellery, an unusual shirt or even a tattoo, something distinctive that tells a story about the person - items like these give you a starting point for conversation. You might even talk about the car park, the traffic to the venue or even the venue proper. Statements like "wow that is a beautiful pendant", "the venue is fantastic" or "nice shirt you are wearing" are some of the statements you can make to attract the other person. Avoid anything too intimate as a starting point or you are likely to offend the other person. As you receive a response, the key is to have something else to say that will give a common platform on which to build a conversation and a relationship. Before you start, you will want to think of a follow up story. This is the key to building a conversation.

Follow up with something and somewhat personal that relates to the other person and that tells them something interesting about you for example:

"I love the color of your shirt, in fact today is the second time I am seeing this color combination, the last time was in a high street shop in London."

This statement helps to connect you to the other person and keeps the conversation moving.

Trying the old standby is another way of starting a conversation.

"Have we met somewhere before?"

Given the right approach and circumstances, this conversation starter can work, for example if you say to someone;

"You look familiar" , "Have I met you before".

This statement makes it easier to put together a lot of infrastructure to start a conversation.

"What college do you attend, I use to be a good footballer those days in the college, and do you do any sporting activity?"

As you go through the details of the other person's life story, you should feel free to go off. Remember, you don't really want to find out if you've met before; you want to get to know each other.

Finally you can make a funny comment which is one of the best ways to start a conversation, you can make comments on the environment e.g. car parking, weather, or the venue - "hey I saw a truck parked in the car park", "Is it just me or is the guy in the front row asleep". The goal is not to be mean -spirited or judgmental, so be sure to keep your comments light-hearted. Try to invite the other person in on the joke. "Who owns the truck parked in the car park" or "Do you think he is going to sleep all through the conference?" Know that this method might be risky. Hence it is difficult with an audience whom you don't know well; however, if you find someone that shares your sense of humor, chances are that it will be the start of a great friendship.

Please remember that some of these trials might fail, if you don't get a positive response from somebody, there are other people you can approach. If you are persistent you will find that over time it will get easier to speak with people. As you become more confident and at ease, you will need to rely on tricks to start conversations.

If you have severe social anxiety disorder, you will also need to receive proper treatment, such as cognitive behavioral therapy or medication. Without effective treatment, tricks such as those conversation starters or other social skill strategies are likely not to be effective.

However it is your responsibility to start a conversation with some talk by calming your nerves with someone equally about some general issues like the venue, the parking, the weather or the refreshment. By doing this you will not blame yourself that you have missed an opportunity.

"Do you know that those who open their mouth and speak are often the ones that make things happen? Get connected by networking with people and take your business to a greater height."

CHAPTER FOUR

Show Interest

To show interest is to be interested in whatever interest you i.e. you've got to find what's interesting in every thing, you've got to be good at noticing things, you've got to be good at listening. If you find people and things interesting, they will find you interesting.

Interesting people are good at sharing; you can't be interested in someone who won't tell you anything. Being good at sharing is not the same as talking, talking, talking on and on. It means you share ideas, you let people play with them and you're good at talking about them without having to talk about yourself.

There are various ways of getting interested in whatever you do. For example, taking picture at least one everyday, start a blog and write at least one sentence, keep a scrap book, read at least a magazine you've never read before, once a month interview someone for 20 minutes, or work out how to make them interesting, collect something, once a week sit in a coffee shop or café for an hour and listen to other people conversation, take notes but be careful at people's privacy. Every month, write 50 words about piece of visual art, one piece of writing, one piece of music, and one piece of TV.

For the benefit of this book, I shall explain with the example of:

'interviewing someone for 20 minutes and work how to make them interesting'.

Again being interesting is about being interested. Interviewing is about making the other person the star, finding out what they know or think that is interesting, could be anyone, a friend, a colleague, a stranger or anyone. Find out what is compelling about them.

Showing interest in whatever you do can help you in preparing yourself for a presentation or talking to someone face to face, thus increasing your chances of making new friendship which can lead to a patronage of your product/services. It can also lead to associationship in the first place.

Talking to somebody is about what you do and how you do it everyday when you interact with other people. At the most basic level, when you have a face to face conversation with someone, you present yourself by your tone of voice, your look, use of words and body language. In other to have effective communication or perhaps passing a message to other people in form of your own point of view, you need to do it with a passion.

In the business world, networking takes on a larger dimension of communication. There are ways of networking where you may speak to a group of fellow business colleagues, associates, executives, clients or customers.

First impression counts and yet your first impression is most important, it is the one that will permeate the entire discussion. Make a first positive impression, and it can cancel out some minor goof-ups you might have made while talking or make a first negative impression and it can cancel out many of the excellent things you must have said during the discussion.

There are rules for making a good impression and only if the rules are abided with, first impression may lead to a fantastic way of networking. The rule are thus:

1. Do not be late for appointment. Being there 20 minutes ahead of time is even better, because it gives you time to shift gears, do any last minutes preparation, perhaps rehearse a little and focus on what and how you're going to go about it.

2. Do not dress like a fashion model. Be neat and clean, just wear clean clothes. Look like you own a business, use good taste and lean towards the conservative side, color and style wise. You will be attractive and unlikely to offend anybody.

3. Take care of personal hygiene; use a moderate perfume to clear away any odors. Ladies do not paint your face with too much color, let your make up be moderate and acceptable corporately.

4. Do not smoke or drink alcohol that might affect your reasonability or personality.

5. Men should have a clean shave or well presented beard. Some people mistrust men with facial hair.

The bottom line of these actions is that you are the actor or actress playing yourself, if you are not interested in what you are doing to be interested in them, you might not be able to network properly to achieving an award winning performance of which the potential reward will be having your prospect say yes I am excited and interested.

CHAPTER FIVE

ALWAYS GIVE

Giving is unique and when you generously give, you share the message of generosity, multiply the joy and give rise to a revolution of happiness. This reminds me of the biblical saying;

"There is blessing in giving than in receiving".

Look for ways, how you can help others, think deeply and you will find out that this action of giving will surely help you to network properly. For example, give advice, referrals, even friendship instead of focusing on selling to people you meet for the first time as this will naturally follow after networking with the person.

Generally speaking, giving is an act that requires giving something out to another person i.e. material, words of wisdom, time, information or otherwise. Giving generously is when you form the habit of giving freely without expecting a return from the person receiving. This free giving can be offering your time, assets, or talent to aid someone in need.

On the other hand, a gift is the transferring of something without the expectation of receiving something in return. Although gift giving might involve an expectation of reciprocal, a gift is meant to be free.

Generously giving and gift are the same for the purpose of networking properly. I will lay more emphasis on generosity which can be spending time, money or labor for others without being rewarded in return.

The term generosity often goes hand in hand with charity and philanthropy. Many people in the public eye who want recognition for their good deeds do give generously to show their contribution, however generosity should not be limited to times of great need or extreme situations but should be practiced by networkers all the time.

Generosity is not solely based on giving money, items, or one's economic status but instead, it should include the individual pure intentions by giving from the heart. So as a passionate net worker, always give from your heart good business advice, referral and friendship.

I was at a social event and met with somebody who was in need of a professional marketer to give an advice on start up business marketing. He informed me of his intention about taking his products to the next level, obviously he will require the services of a professional marketer, business startup professional and so on, name it. These services are not free, but could be given free through networking with people. As a professional marketer and also a net worker, all I did was to give him a little tutorial on the production of flyers distribution process.

Obviously, his business was relatively small at that time and with minimal capital situation. The advice, however, led to his breakthrough. I gave the tutorial generously.

I never expected a return from this business. But because we have been able to network for this success, we became close and a business relationship developed and I became his marketing consultant. Today the business has grown from strength to strength.

"There is something in you that the whole world needs. Find it, develop it, and give it through networking with people."

CHAPTER SIX

KEEP YOUR MIND OPEN

Keeping an open mind aid good decision making. Being receptive to new and different ideas or considering the opinion of others helps to determine your mind at making decisions which can also be determined by having a tolerant to liberal views.

However, Aristotle once said "it is the mark of an educated mind to be able to entertain a thought without accepting it". Listening to others ideas may not be easy, but it could be a valuable way to learn something new or change your perspective of reasoning to life issue.

Keeping one's mind open is the beginning of wisdom in reaction to networking with people i.e. you must resist the urge to discuss a contact if they don't seem to fit your needs because you never know when you will need them in future.

Thinking right towards people is a basic rule for winning success. If you open your mind and remember the contact, you might need the support of the contact in the near future. The only hurdle between you and what you want to achieve for your business is the support of others.

Let us look at it this way. For example a business thrives because it has the patronage of people; if they don't patronize the business, obviously the business will fail and go into liquidation or closes down. A politician depends on voters to elect him or she to office, a writer depends on people to read what he or she writes, and a salesman or woman depends on people to buy the product.

It is living in the past when a person can gain a position of authority with force and remain in that position by force e.g. a Military Government (Dictatorship). In those days, the leader has the control of the government and the people or the governed either cooperate with him by force or get jailed or put in detention.

But today and in a civilized situation, a person can get into a position of authority through the support of people only. You just have to seek the support of people through electioneering campaign or canvassing for support to succeed through networking with people and to do that, you must think right towards people.

Successful people follow a plan for liking people or better put linking people by networking. Every friend you make lifts you just one notch higher and being likeable makes you lighter to lift. Take for example a person is not pulled up to a higher position, rather he or she is lifted up through recommendations and in most cases that person must have been known by the person recommending through networking. The individual is chosen whose record stands higher than the rest.

Learn to remember names and contacts because inefficiency at this point of networking may indicate that your interest is not sufficiently out-going. Cultivate the quality of being interesting so people will get something of value from their association with you. Acquire the quality of relaxed easy going so that things do not annoy you while studying to get the 'scratchy'elements out of your personality even those of which you may be unconscious of.

Never miss an opportunity to say a word of thanks to anyone who gives you a compliment and be a comfortable person so that there will be no strain in being with you. Be an old-shoe, old hat kind of individual.

If you do the above and practice liking people until you learn to do so genuinely, you will become a passionate business networker and the success of your business is guaranteed - all other factors being equal. However, you will also need to accomplish this by applying the following principles.

1. A willingness to hear others opinion - the ability to voluntarily hear others opinion by being cooperative and enthusiastic.

2. Give enough time for the expression of opinion - the ability to give adequate time for the listening of others opinion e.g. as much as you need or as many as can be tolerated.

3. Always be patient with people - the ability to endure waiting, delay or provocation without becoming annoyed or upset. To persevere calmly when faced with difficulty.

4. The ability to bite your tongue - rather than rise to somebody's bait by responding when somebody tries to get you involved in a scheme or an argument.

"You will succeed in everything you set your mind on, keep an open mind and never give up on networking with people."

CHAPTER SEVEN

FOLLOW-UP

Follow-up is often defined as the act or an instance of follow up as to further an end or review new developments after the initial contact. It can also be defined as a continuation either by further action, investigation, or a subsequent event that result from and is intended to supplement something done before. Follow-up is often as important as the initial contact in gaining new clients through networking. However, if you have promised somebody information, a referral or a phone number, make sure you follow-up to do the needful or you risk damaging your reputation.

Follow-up is also important in the medical world, for *example*: the social worker emphasis on follow-up to reassure her clients or an intended follow-up to reinforce or evaluate previous actions e.g. follow-up examination after the surgery. In the media world, a report or an article giving further information on a previously reported or written item can also be called a follow-up.

Let us look at a simple follow-up formula designed and formulated by my humble selves thus: a+m+b=1. This formula works with the guiding principle of: if and only if the procedure of having the right attitude, making reference and right behavior is used then the formula will apply e.g.

Attitude = contacting the other person.

Making reference = who, where, how and what was discussed.

Behavior = having the right attitude

Therefore a+m+b=1

Please note, this formula is derived from the principle of marriage, whereby 1+1=1

A friend who was having problem with follow-up once shared his experience with me and I discovered that he was not using the right procedure of follow up, rather each time he made his contact he did not apply the formula as contained in the procedure of follow-up. Rather, he choose the wrong procedure. The problem was that every single message he was writing was the same with the necessary input, to me it was really boring in my opinion. For example as contained in his note:

"Hi,

It was a pleasure to meet you at the meeting this weekend and I hope we can meet again soon."

Regards

There was no reference as to who, where, how, or what they have discussed earlier since they met or what they could do together in the future. The problem is that he had no idea of what to say when he was following-up and this was his weak point which will definitely be a barrier for him to follow-up appropriately.

The following are the ideas I generated to support my friend and every other person who might be having a similar problem of following-up after getting connected through networking.

1. Setting a foundation for follow-up while you are talking. In fact follow-up starts when the conversation starts. During the conversation be looking for something to say in your follow-up. As soon at it hits you make a note of it on the back of their business card or flyer if available. You can find something in common, a topic of interest, whether personal or professional or listen for what they might need help with, then, in your follow-up offer an idea, a contact, or recommend someone to the person.

2. Follow-up right away to build on the momentum of the conversation of your freshness in their mind. If too much time passes before you follow-up, the conversation may slip into the recess of their mind or

blur with that of someone else they met recently, if you wait, it won't have a strong impact. Do it the next day if possible or at the very least sometime before the week is out.

3. Use persuasive copy writing in your follow-up. Strive to incorporate persuasion in all of your communications, that includes your follow-up because its all about promoting your products and services to anyone and everyone you come in contact with.

The most effective follow-up highlights the benefit of working with you, at least having something to give (see chapter five). Here is a follow-up I gave my friend considering the above mentioned factors.

Dear James,

It was a pleasure to meet you at the meeting last week. I am sure I can help you create a business start up plan. The marketing mentoring program of guiding angels would be an effective way to that because it provides the three things you need most for your business.

A PLAN- We shall create a marketing plan that is tailored to your needs.

ACCOUNTABILITY - I will keep you well informed with our weekly e-mails.

FEED BACKS - You won't waste time and money like the beginners do, as I will help you avoid mistakes beginners make.

I will call you next week to continue these conversations. Regards

Follow this simple formula and state what you can do with confidence, list at least three things they will get and the benefit of each, then close with a testimonial and a way to keep in touch. By doing this, your networking effort will be the foundation for a healthy business that brings you more contract and more clients than ever imagined.

"Press on, nothing in this world can stop you from following up on networking with people even talents will not because it's the best way to a win win situation."

CHAPTER EIGHT

Retain And Build Relationship

Retaining and building relationship is the key to your personal success, hence successful people have the ability to develop relationship that last. Building relationship requires the building of trust, be consistent and regularly attend events so that you become known to all.

Relationship can not stand if it lacks trust. Mutual trust is shared belief that you can depend on each other to achieve a common purpose. More comprehensively trust is the willingness of a party (trustor) to be vulnerable to the actions of another party (trustee) based on the expectation that the trustee will perform an action important to the trustor regardless of the trustor's ability to monitor or control the trustee. For the purpose of clarity, the words trustor / trustee is a person or group of persons acting in a position of confidence in and reliance on good qualities especially fairness, trust, honor, or ability. It can also be said to be a position of obligation by somebody who is expected by others to behave reasonably and responsibly.

A relationship is two or more people eliciting responses from each other. If you want a change in response then you must change your own response to a workable response with others. For example as a business owner or business professional, you should ask yourself this simple question,'what business am I into?' The answer is quite simple and if your business has anything to do with people, as all businesses do, then you are in the business of building relationship. Some people think that if they sell things, they are in the business of selling but they are not, they are actually in the business of building relationship because that is how you sell to make more profit, if the relationship is right and well above expectation.

There is a friendship factor in building relationship because in today's customer driven economy, business owners and organizations must move from product - based campaign marketing to a customer - focused personalized approach. People want to feel important and they also want to know that you have expertise with their life or work issue. The more you demonstrate your specific of their problems, concerns, and aspiration, the more quickly they will buy from you often without really understanding what you are selling.

Those in management are also in the business of building relationship, because that is how you get things done. Management is more art than science.

Moreover, managing is working with people and through other people to accomplish the objectives of both organization and its members. Management consist of the rational assessment of a situation and the systematic selection of goals and purpose i.e. what is to be done in relationship to developing strategies of achieving organizational goals. Management also consist of the marshalling of the required resources as to rational design, organization, direction and control of the activities required to attain the selected purposes and finally the motivating and rewarding of people to do the work.

Effective listen broaden us, lay the groundwork for peace, elevate the quality of our relationship and open way to success, if nothing else, when you listen, you will find you are the most important person in the room. Listening isn't easy, if it were everyone would do it. Most of us think we are born listener just because our ears work, That is just like this notable quote which states that:

"you are a born pianist because your family had a piano in the house "-Linda Eve Diamonds

Building a relationship involves all the peaceful act of being a good listener and applying the ten rules of listening which are : stop talking, create a space, be orderly, respect others, hold your judgment, don't be a label reader, open your mind, remain focused, ask questions, and be aware of the speaker.

The purpose of a business is to create and keep a customer, if a business successfully creates and keep a customer in a cost effective way, that business will make profit while conforming to survive and thrive. If for any reason a business fails to attract or sustain a sufficient number of customers, it will experience losses and too many losses will lead to the demise of the business. Hence customer based approach will foster good relationship which will give rise to success of the business.

"Keep on multiplying relationships for good through networking with people, as there is no substitute for hard work in the school of success."

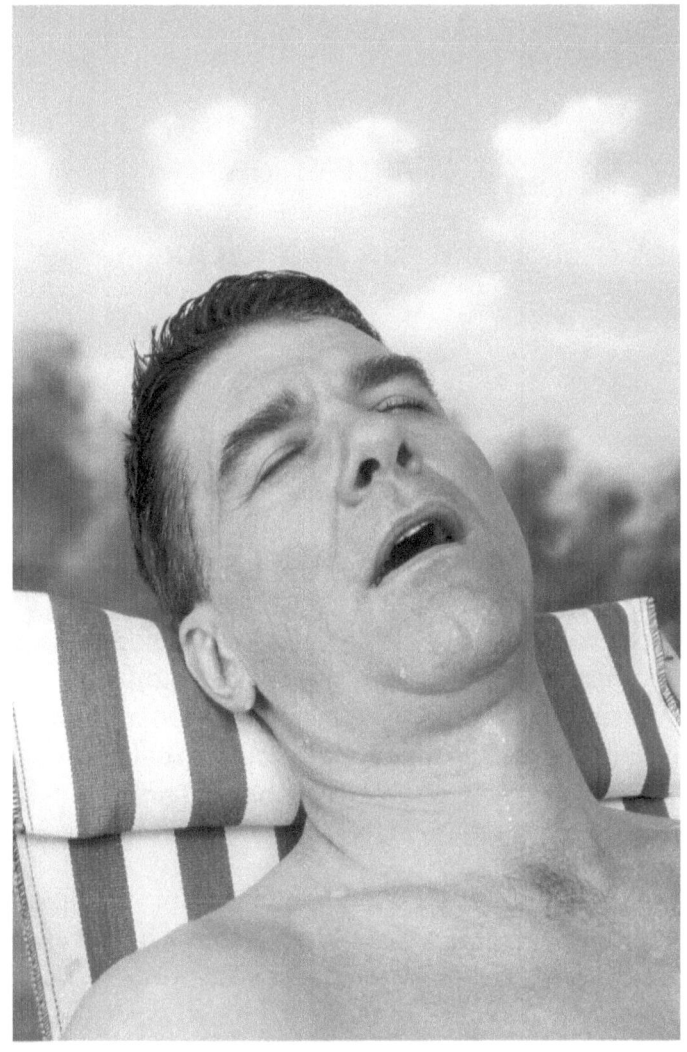

CHAPTER NINE

Have fun and relax

Having fun and relaxing are two words that can be equal to "a recess from the responsibility of life by making time for yourself for recreational activities". The strategies of having fun is by nurturing your feelings or sense of humour to looking at the light side of your concerns at least for a while and keep on enjoying yourself. This is a specific recommendation of life style because it discourages having depression or loneliness. The barrier to this strategy is poor time management or over serious attitude to life.

Events and social gathering are places for having fun and relaxing. All you need to do is to remain focused and be yourself. It is a place where absolute networking will take place, so relax and keep on networking, keep on knowing and getting noticed by people because you are about to break even by knowing somebody who might be the one to turn around your fortune.

Researches have confirmed that people perform best when they are in relaxed and comfortable situation. So relax and have fun. From sport to nuclear physics, people get the best performance in the task given them when they are relaxed, with intent on what they're doing and more of less obvious of everything else, when they are having fun, so loosen up and enjoy your networking with people.

There are principles of having fun and in applying these principles you will be relaxed at networking with people.

Firstly, you must stop hiding who you are. Let people know who you are, because it will eventually affect your business if the person you are dealing with discovers that you are not the same person he or she had discussion with. Just be honest and be truthful at introducing who you are, because personal identity forms the basis of having to do business with you. For example;

"Is this person a fit and proper person to do business or transact business with?"

Obviously the answer to this question will definitely determine the on-going of that transaction.

Secondly, start something probably a small talk, this will trigger a wider discussion and by doing this a foundation of your getting connected with others automatically will be activated. You can imagine if at an event nobody talks to each other, definitely there will be a grave- like situation, just like the land of the deaths and there will be no connection as to networking.

Thirdly, don't worry about what others think about you, be passionate about your aims and objectives as networking is getting connected with people and you must realize that you can not be stopped or else the purpose of attending that gathering or occasion will be defeated. Think about it and be serious about it, then you will be connected.

Fourth, stop taking it so damn seriously, this principle enables you to get going even if you talk to somebody and you 're ignored , you have to move on by talking to the next person who might have felt bad about the way you were treated by the earlier person and on sympathy ground decides to talk to you. Because you have kept your head high even at that embarrassing situation, that you did not take that action seriously might get you connected as you will be seen as a person who is focused at his objective of attending the social occasion.

Fifth, stop being busy, this principle helps you to forge ahead in networking your business because the atmosphere you find yourself in is a relaxing situation where you must forget about being busy and start by talking to people and making the best use of the situation.

"Don't worry about tomorrow, because tomorrow might not come. Today is all yours, just relax and have fun while networking with people."

CHAPTER TEN

BECOME A PASSIONATE NETWORKER

It is a fact that 80% of all new businesses is gained through referrals or relationship marketing that is achievable through networking with people, and not only that, it is one of the most cost effective ways of building business.

You may already have spent considerable time, effort and money on other marketing methods such as advertising or direct mailing with little or no return. Perhaps you have tried cold-calling with little to show for your effort leaving you feeling demoralized and unhappy.

Look no further; apply the principle of networking whereby you attend events like social gathering, conferences, dinner, and sports outing where you can meet with people to network.

Becoming a passionate networker has the advantage of excelling in business and building relationship. This brings us to the topic 'passionate networker'and the question 'what makes one to be a passionate networker?

What makes one to be passionate about networking is the people in it and those who are passionate about what they do, passionate about supporting people, and helping others to excel in their business endeavors. It is then about harnessing this passion to generate a genuine interest in each other, developing a meaningful relationship and ultimately generating business.

To achieve the above, the fallowing points should be considered.

Provide an opportunity to understand each other's passion and expertise through meaningful discussion by way of networking.

Inviting others to come and join in an event where networking will take place.

Generating interesting discussions that will span through business and social topics which really do help us to understand the real person behind the name.

Proactively looking to help others by making appropriate introduction, referrals, and giving unconditional help and support.

"The quality of your followership is determined by your type of management."

WHERE TO FIND AN APPROPRIATE BUSINESS NETWORKING EVENTS IN THE UK

- The Chartered Institute of Marketing www.cim.co.uk/events
- Business link Northwest www.businesslink.gov.uk
- The Manchester African Business Forum www.mabfonline.com
- Chartered Management Institute www.managers.org.uk
- Institute of Directors www.iod.com
- Chambers of Commerce in the UK e.g. www.gmchamber.co.uk
- Institute of Business Advisers www.iba.org.uk
- Institute of Leadership & Management www.i-l-m.com
- Learn Direct for Business www.learndirect-business.co.uk
- New Business – New Life www.newbusiness-newlife.org.uk

WATCH OUT FOR OUR NEXT PUBLICATION
BUILDING YOUR BUSINESS WITH NETWORK
MARKETING

An innovative approach to positive thinking in
business management

ABOUT THE AUTHOR

Lucky Okome is a Chartered Marketer and a regional board member of the Chartered Institute of Marketing Northwest England. In addition to this, he is an Executive Director of Manchester African Business Forum Limited and self employed business owner of Italo Marketing Solutions. Lucky is into Mentoring and Coaching with Community and Development Partners Blackburn as a volunteer to give something back to the community.

Lucky holds a masters degree in Business Administration (MBA) specializing in Marketing Management and also an HND in Statistics.

Lucky's belief in networking prompts the birth of this book which will bring a break through to exciting new levels of success at business and in life.

He is married to Oluwafunmilayo and they have two sons Oluwaseun Tobore and Oluwafemi Oghenekevwe. They reside in the United Kingdom.